easy cut-up
cakes
FOR KIDS

easy cut-up cakes
FOR KIDS

melissa barlow

Gibbs Smith, Publisher

TO ENRICH AND INSPIRE HUMANKIND

Salt Lake City | Charleston | Santa Fe | Santa Barbara

For Todd and our little angels

First Edition
11 10   20 19 18 17 16 15 14 13 12 11 10 9 8 7 6 5 4 3

Published by
Gibbs Smith, Publisher
P.O. Box 667
Layton, Utah 84041

Orders: 1.800.835.4993
www.gibbs-smith.com

Designed by Dawn DeVries Sokol
Manufactured in Hong Kong in May 2010 by Paramount Printing Company Ltd.

Library of Congress Cataloging-in-Publication Data

Barlow, Melissa.
  Easy cut-up cakes for kids / Melissa Barlow ; photographs by Zachary Williams.— 1st ed.
     p. cm.
  ISBN-13: 978-1-4236-0175-3
  ISBN-10: 1-4236-0175-0
  1. Cookery. I. Title.

TX652.5.B227 2007
641.5—dc22
                    2006102581

contents

introduction

Now you can bake and decorate your very own *fun shape cake!* This book is full of easy cake ideas that you can make for birthdays or other special occasions. Choose from bugs, animals, and silly shapes to surprise your family and friends with your creative genius!

READY, SET . . .

Before you start baking, please do two very important things:

    1. Ask permission from your parent or guardian.

    2. Find an adult helper to join you in the fun—mainly to keep you safe, but also to answer questions you might have about the recipe or ingredients. In this book you will use electric mixers, hot ovens, and knives. You need an adult helper and must always be careful!

GO BAKE!

The first step when making any recipe in this book is to *read the whole recipe first.* Search the cupboards to make sure you have the right pans for the cake you've chosen. Then gather all the ingredients together so they will be handy.

    Now turn on the oven to the temperature noted in the recipe. Let the oven preheat (reach the desired temperature) while you grease the cake pans and mix

the batter. An oven that has been preheated will cook the cake evenly. And pans that have been well greased will let the cake pop out in one piece after it has cooled a bit.

After mixing the ingredients together and making a deliciously smooth batter, carefully transfer the batter to the greased pans. Then your adult helper can help you carefully put the pans into the oven. Set a timer and then relax until it rings, dings, or whistles at you. To test for doneness, have your adult helper insert a toothpick in the center of the cake. If it comes out clean, the cake is done.

Let cakes cool completely before you frost them. This will help keep crumbs out of your frosting. You can even bake the cake a day before you'll need it.

LET'S FROST

Frosting is one of the most important parts of decorating your cake. Frosting can be messy, so be very careful as you decorate and ask your adult helper to work with you.

To help keep *you* clean, wear an apron. To help keep *your cake plate* clean, stick little pieces of wax paper just under the edges of your cake. Then your cake plate won't have frosting all over it. When you finish frosting the cake, just pull out the wax paper pieces and throw them away.

What Frosting Should I Use?

There are many yummy flavors of frosting that you can buy. These are usually whipped, making them easy to spread. Sometimes you need frosting that is stiffer, such as for squeezing through a decorating bag to draw lines or make shapes. For stiffer frosting (or if you want to flavor it yourself), you and your adult helper can make these easy recipes instead of buying frosting from the store:

VANILLA BUTTERCREAM FROSTING

1 stick margarine or butter, softened*

3 to 4 tablespoons water or milk

2 teaspoons vanilla*

Pinch salt (optional)

1 pound powdered sugar (about 4 cups)

Beat margarine or butter, water or milk, and vanilla together with an electric hand mixer until smooth. Add salt, if using. Gradually beat in the powdered sugar, 1 cup at a time. If the frosting is too thick, add more water or milk by the teaspoon until it reaches the right consistency. If it is too thin, add a little more powdered sugar.

*Substitute 1 cup regular vegetable shortening and clear vanilla if you want a more pure white, less cream-colored frosting.

Chocolate Frosting

1 stick margarine or butter, softened

3 to 4 tablespoons water or milk

2 teaspoons vanilla

Pinch salt (optional)

1/2 cup cocoa powder

3 to 4 cups powdered sugar

Beat margarine or butter, water or milk, and vanilla together with an electric hand mixer until smooth. Add salt, if using. Beat in cocoa powder. Gradually beat in the powdered sugar, 1 cup at a time. If the frosting is too thick, add more water or milk by the teaspoon until it reaches the right consistency. If it is too thin, add a little more powdered sugar.

What Is Tube Frosting?

You can buy frosting at the grocery store that comes in tubes. You might want to use these instead of decorator bags. They are great to use for decorating and adding details to your cakes. The tubes come in small and large sizes. The small tubes are usually filled with gel frosting and the large tubes come with regular frosting. Both kinds come in all colors of the rainbow and are very easy to use.

How Do I Color My Frosting?

Most grocery stores have food-coloring kits somewhere on the cake aisle. These work well, but sometimes the colors aren't as deep or dark as you'd like them to be. You and your adult helper may want to go to a craft store and buy some Wilton Icing Colors. They are not expensive and will help you get the exact color you need. If there isn't a craft store near you that carries Wilton products, some chain stores do, like Wal-Mart, or you can visit their website at www.wilton.com to look for products and icing colors available online. Just remember to be careful when using any coloring, because it will stain your clothes!

LET'S DECORATE

Now comes the best part. You can choose to decorate your cake with your favorite candy and other treats! You don't have to use exactly what is listed in each recipe, just remember it's best to use bright, colorful candy.

A lot of recipes call for different types of snack cakes to use when decorating. For example, your cake may call for mini donuts or Oreos that are then used for wheels on a car or train, or Twinkies cut in half that are used for legs on a turtle. Use what you think sounds best.

Just remember that the most important thing is to be creative and have fun. The possibilities are endless!

freddy
the froggy

1. Make cake mix according to package directions. Fill two cups in the cupcake pan about two-thirds full. Pour half of the remaining batter into the square pan and the other half into the round pan. Bake cupcakes and cakes at 350 degrees F for 20 to 23 minutes and then carefully remove cupcakes from oven. Continue baking the cakes until done, according to directions on box. Cool cakes in pans for 10 minutes, and then invert and cool completely on a wire rack.

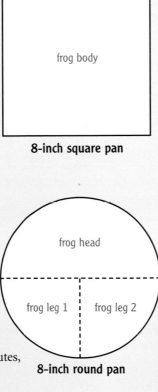

8-inch square pan

frog body

8-inch round pan

frog head

frog leg 1 | frog leg 2

PANS: Cupcake pan
   1 (8-inch) square pan
   1 (8-inch) round pan

1 cake mix, any flavor

Bright green frosting

White frosting

2 chocolate chips or mini Oreo
   cookies

1 piece red licorice

1 tube red gel frosting or red
   Fruit by the Foot

10 green or white mini
   marshmallows

1 tube black gel frosting

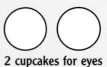

2 cupcakes for eyes

SERVES: 10 to 12

11

2. Cut the round cake according to the diagram on page 11. Place the square cake on a plate or foil-wrapped board. Place half of the round cake at the top for the frog's head. Put the cut pieces of cake with the round side out at the bottom of the square to make the frog's legs.

3. Frost the entire cake smooth with green or yellow frosting. Frost the sides of the cupcakes green and the tops of the cupcakes white. Set the cupcakes at the top of the frog's head for eyes. Place an upside-down chocolate chip or a mini Oreo cookie in the center of each.

4. Cut the ends off the licorice and then put on the frog's face in the shape of a smile. Use the red gel frosting or a piece of Fruit by the Foot to create the tongue. Finally, place 5 mini marshmallows along the bottom of each of the frog's feet to create toes. Draw an arch with the black gel frosting above the marshmallows on each side to finish the frog's feet.

flutterby

1. Make cake mix according to package directions. Bake cake as directed on box for two round pans. Cool cakes in pans for 10 minutes, and then invert and cool completely on a wire rack.

2. Cut both layers of cake according to the diagram.

3. Arrange one of the rectangular pieces on the middle of a plate or foil-wrapped board. Frost the top, and then place the second rectangular layer on top. Frost the entire body with pink frosting.

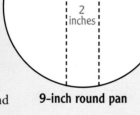

9-inch round pan

4. Place one layer of the wings on each side of the butterfly body. Frost the top, and then place the second wing layer on top. Frost the top and sides carefully with pink frosting.

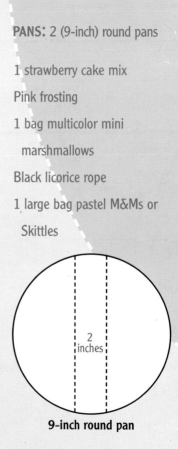

PANS: 2 (9-inch) round pans

1 strawberry cake mix

Pink frosting

1 bag multicolor mini
   marshmallows

Black licorice rope

1 large bag pastel M&Ms or
   Skittles

9-inch round pan

SERVES: 10 to 12

5. Open the mini marshmallows, and separate the pink marshmallows from the rest in the bag. Using a pair of kitchen scissors, cut the pink marshmallows in half lengthwise. You may not need to use them all, so cut them in batches. Place marshmallow halves, cut side down, over entire butterfly body (not the wings). Cut two pieces of the licorice rope and stick down through the marshmallows into the cake for the antennae.

6. Finally, sort out the colors of the candy you're using for the wings, making sure to incorporate some pink to match the body. Arrange a pattern on the countertop to make sure you have enough of every color you're using. Transfer pattern to the cake.

Note: You can change the color scheme easily by using a different color of frosting and mini marshmallows for the body. For example, try yellow frosting with the yellow mini marshmallows.

Variation: Make two single-layer butterflies instead of one double-layer butterfly.

clown fish

1. Make cake mix according to package directions. Bake cake as directed on box for a 9 x 13-inch pan. Cool cake in pan for 10 minutes, and then invert and cool completely on a wire rack.

2. Cut the cake according to the diagram.

3. Put the top fin in place, and then frost entire cake with orange frosting. Position the side fin near the center and frost with orange frosting.

PANS: 1 (9 x 13-inch) pan

1 white or orange cake mix
Orange frosting
White frosting
1 tube black gel frosting
1 mini Oreo
1 brown M&M

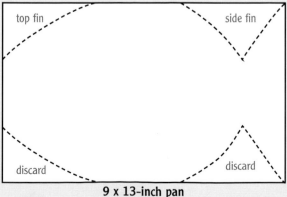

top fin   side fin

discard   discard

9 x 13-inch pan

SERVES: 10 to 12

4. Using the white frosting in a decorator's bag with a round or star tip, carefully zigzag three thick lines on the fish's body starting at the top and then working your way across to the bottom.

5. Outline the white stripes with the black tube frosting. Also put a black stripe along the tail, top fin, and side fin as shown in the photo.

6. Carefully pull apart the Oreo. Using the side with the cream filling, position the Oreo, cream filling up, as the eye. Put brown M&M in center for the pupil. Use black tube frosting to draw on a smile.

slow poke

PANS: 1 (2.5-quart) glass
mixing bowl
Cupcake pan

1 chocolate cake mix

Chocolate frosting

Green frosting

2 Twinkies

1 large tube green frosting

Candy for decorating

1. Make cake mix according to package directions. Fill two cups in the cupcake pan about two-thirds full. Pour remaining batter into a well-greased mixing bowl. Bake cupcakes and cake at 350 degrees F for 20 to 23 minutes and then carefully remove cupcakes from oven. Bake cake another 25 to 30 minutes, or until done. Test by inserting a wooden skewer in the center; if it comes out clean, the cake is done. Cool cake in bowl for 10 minutes, and then invert and cool completely on a wire rack.

2. Place the cooled cake with the rounded side up on a plate or foil-wrapped board. Frost the entire cake with chocolate frosting.

3. Slice off the tops of cooled cupcakes; discard or eat the bottoms. Spread a little frosting on the cut side of the cupcake tops, and then place frosted sides together to make the turtle's head. Frost one side of the head with some of the green

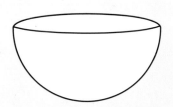

2 cupcakes

SERVES: 10 to 12   **2.5-quart glass mixing bowl**

20

frosting, and then stick it on the front of the turtle. Finish frosting the head green.

4. Cut each Twinkie in half and position as legs around the turtle shell. Frost with green frosting.

5. Finally, using the tube frosting or a decorator's bag with a star tip, draw lines according to the picture to create the shell's pattern. Position the candy to make the turtle's face.

Variation: Instead of making the turtle brown with green highlights, you can frost the entire turtle with some dark green mint-flavored frosting and use black or brown tube frosting to draw the lines.

teddy bear

PANS: 1 (2.5-quart) glass
mixing bowl
Cupcake pan

1 chocolate cake mix

Chocolate frosting

1 tube red or light brown
  frosting

1 tube black gel frosting

Red rope licorice (optional)

2 Oreo cookies

2 Hershey s kisses

Red Fruit by the Foot

3 cupcakes

SERVES: 10 to 12

2.5-quart glass mixing bowl

1. Make cake mix according to package directions. Fill three cups in the cupcake pan about two-thirds full. Pour remaining batter into a well-greased mixing bowl. Bake cupcakes and cake at 350 degrees F for 20 to 23 minutes and then carefully remove cupcakes from oven. Bake cake another 25 to 30 minutes, or until done. Test by inserting a wooden skewer in the center; if it comes out clean, the cake is done. Cool cake in bowl for 10 minutes, and then invert and cool completely on a wire rack.

2. Place the cooled cake with the rounded side up on your plate or foil-wrapped board. Frost the entire cake with chocolate frosting.

3. Frost two cupcakes, and place at the top of the head for the bear's ears. Slice off the top of the remaining cupcake; eat or throw away the bottom. Place the cupcake top slightly above the center of the bear's face to create the nose; frost and blend with the frosting on the bear's face.

4. Using the red or light brown frosting, fill in a circle in the middle of each ear. Draw a nose on the cupcake top using the black gel frosting. Use red rope licorice to make the mouth, or you can use the red tube frosting.

5. Separate two Oreos and place with the cream filling facing up to make the eyes. Place upside down Hershey's kisses in the center. You might need to cut off the tips so the kisses lay flat.

6. You can make a bow tie out of red Fruit by the Foot if you like.

chilly igloo

PANS: 1 (2.5-quart) glass
mixing bowl

1 white or chocolate cake mix

White frosting

2 Ding Dongs

1 bag (16 ounces) white

marshmallows

SERVES: 10 to 12

1. Make cake mix according to package directions.
Pour batter into a well-greased mixing bowl. Bake at
350 degrees F for 54 to
59 minutes. Test by
inserting a wooden
skewer in the center; if
it comes out clean, the
cake is done. Cool
cake in bowl for 10
minutes, and then
invert and cool completely on a wire rack.

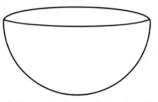
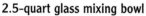

2.5-quart glass mixing bowl

2. Place the cooled cake with the rounded side up
on a plate or foil-wrapped board. Frost the entire
cake white.

3. Cut off and discard the bottom third of the Ding
Dongs so they can stand on their sides. Frost the
Ding Dong pieces together and then place against
the frosted cake for the igloo's door. Completely
frost Ding Dongs with white frosting and blend into
sides of igloo.

4. Start cutting marshmallows in half lengthwise with a pair of kitchen scissors. Place each, cut side down, into the frosting, starting on one side of the doorway at the bottom and then going all the way around to the other side of the doorway. Follow this pattern until the igloo is completely covered. Once done, cut more marshmallows to cover the outside of the doorway.

Variation: Use whole mini marshmallows instead of large ones.

watermelon

1. Make cake mix according to package directions. Stir in ¾ cup chocolate chips, and bake cake as directed on box for two round pans. Cool cakes in pans for 10 minutes, then invert and cool completely on a wire rack.

2. Place one cake layer in the center of a plate or foil-wrapped board and frost the top with red frosting. Sprinkle some chocolate chips over frosting. Place second cake layer over top, and then frost sides green, and about ¼ inch around the outside edge of the top. You can use a decorator's tip if you like.

3. Frost top of cake with red frosting and smooth. Place some chocolate chips across the top to look like seeds.

PANS: 2 (8- or 9-inch) round pans

1 strawberry cake mix

¾ cup chocolate chips plus more

Red frosting

Green frosting

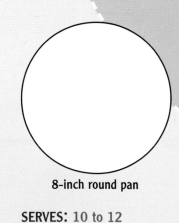

8-inch round pan

SERVES: 10 to 12

8-inch round pan

gumball machine

PANS: 1 (8-inch) round pan
      1 (8-inch) square pan

1 rainbow chip or
  funfetti cake mix

White frosting

Red frosting

1 tube black gel frosting

1 mini Oreo (optional)

Gumballs

SERVES: 10 to 12

1. Make cake mix according to package directions. Bake cake as directed on box for two 8-inch pans. Cool cakes in pans for 10 minutes, and then invert and cool completely on a wire rack.

8-inch round pan

2. Place the square cake at the bottom, and then set the round cake above it to look like a gumball machine. Frost entire round cake white and entire square cake red.

8-inch square pan

3. Using the black gel frosting, draw a rounded arch on the bottom of the square cake to show where the

28

gum would come out of the machine. Fill in this area with black frosting, and then place 2 or 3 gumballs on the frosting. Above the arch, draw a slot where you would insert the money. You can even put a penny in the slot if you want! Place half a mini Oreo above it as in the photo if you would like.

4. Place gumballs evenly and close together all over the white frosting to look as if they are in a gumball machine.

Variation: Make the base of the gumball machine any color you want.

quacky the ducky

PANS: 1 (2.5-quart) glass
mixing bowl
1 (8-inch) round pan

1 lemon cake mix

Yellow or lemon frosting

Orange frosting

2 mini Oreos

1 tube black gel frosting

SERVES: 10 to 12

1. Make cake mix according to package directions. Measure 3 cups batter into a well-greased mixing bowl. Pour remaining batter into greased round pan. Bake cakes at 350 degrees for 30 to 33 minutes. Remove round pan from oven and let cool 10 minutes in pan, then invert and cool completely on a wire rack. Continue baking cake in bowl another 10 to 15 minutes. Test by inserting a wooden skewer in the center; if it comes out clean, the cake is done. Cool cake in bowl for 10 minutes, then invert and cool completely on a wire rack.

2. Cut the round layer in half lengthwise so you have two flat circles. Place one in the center of a plate or

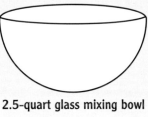

2.5-quart glass mixing bowl

8-inch round pan

foil-wrapped board. Top with the cooled cake from the bowl, and then frost the entire thing yellow.

3. Cut the remaining round cake half into two equal pieces, and stack the cut sides together. This will create the ducky bill. Cut to fit around ducky head and then frost entire bill orange. You can use a decorator's tip to draw a line between the bill and duck's head if you want.

4. Carefully pull apart the 2 Oreos. Using the sides with the cream filling up, position the cookies just above the bill for the eyes. Put a drop of black gel frosting in the center of each cookie to finish the eyes.

Variation: Color some shredded coconut with a drop or two of yellow food coloring in a ziplock bag and sprinkle all over the ducky head after frosting to give him a feathery texture!

football

PANS: 1 (9 x 13-inch) pan

1 chocolate cake mix

Chocolate frosting

1 large tube white frosting

1. Make cake mix according to package directions. Bake cake as directed on box for a 9 x 13-inch pan. Cool cake in pan for 10 minutes, and invert and cool completely on a wire rack.

2. Cut the cake according to the diagram, and throw away or eat the unused pieces.

3. Frost the entire cake with chocolate frosting. Using the white tube frosting or a decorator's bag, draw a white line and then the smaller white lines across it to look like the football laces.

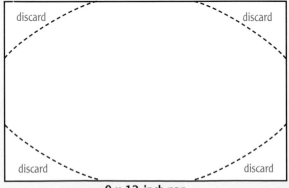

9 x 13-inch pan

SERVES: 8 to 10

32

4. On each end of the football, draw curved white lines for the football stripes.

Variation: Using green tube frosting, create grass around the football by putting the end of the tube right up against the bottom of the football and pulling out while pressing on the tube.

little ladybug

PANS: 1 (2.5-quart) glass
mixing bowl
Cupcake pan

1 cake mix, any flavor

Red frosting

1 to 2 large tubes
black frosting

Black rope licorice

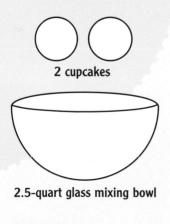

2 cupcakes

2.5-quart glass mixing bowl

SERVES: 10 to 12

1. Make cake mix according to package directions. Fill two cups in the cupcake pan about two-thirds full. Pour remaining batter into a well-greased mixing bowl. Bake cupcakes and cake at 350 degrees for 20 to 23 minutes and then carefully remove cupcakes from oven. Bake cake another 25 to 30 minutes, or until done. Test by inserting a wooden skewer in the center; if it comes out clean, the cake is done. Cool cake in bowl for 10 minutes, then invert and cool completely on a wire rack.

2. Place the cooled cake with the rounded side up on a plate or foil-wrapped board. Frost the entire cake red.

3. Slice off the tops of the cupcakes; throw away or eat the bottoms. Spread a little frosting on the cut side of the cupcake tops and then place frosted sides together to make the ladybug's head. Frost one side of the head with black frosting and then position it on the front of the ladybug. Frost the remainder of the head black.

4. Using the black tube frosting or a decorator's bag with a star tip, zigzag a black line down the center of the ladybug body to make wings. Finish by drawing large black black dots all over the wings. Cut two pieces of licorice rope and stick in the head to make antennae.

Variation: Use Hershey s Kisses for the dots. Just press the tips into the frosting so the round, flat side faces up.

baseball cap

PANS: 1 (2.5-quart) glass
      mixing bowl
      1 (8-inch) round pan

1 cake mix, any flavor

White frosting

Blue or red frosting

1 tube red gel frosting or red
  rope licorice

Blue M&Ms or Skittles

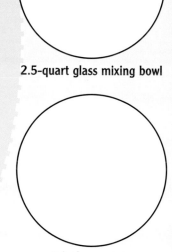

2.5-quart glass mixing bowl

8-inch round pan

1. Make cake mix according to package directions. Measure 3 cups batter into a well-greased mixing bowl. Pour remaining batter into greased round pan. Bake cakes at 350 degrees for 30 to 33 minutes. Remove round pan from oven and let cool 10 minutes in pan, then invert and cool cake completely on a wire rack. Continue baking cake in bowl another 10 to 15 minutes. Test by inserting a wooden skewer in the center; if it comes out clean, the cake is done. Cool cake in bowl for 10 minutes, then invert and cool completely on a wire rack.

2. Cut the round layer in half lengthwise so you have two flat circles. Place one in the center of a plate or

foil-wrapped board. Top with the cooled cake from
the bowl and then frost the entire thing white.

3. Cut the remaining round cake half into two
equal pieces and stack the cut sides together. This
will create the brim of the hat. Cut to fit around the
cap and then frost entire brim blue.

4. Using the tube of red gel frosting or red licorice,
make lines all around the cap as shown in the photo.
On top of the hat in the center, place one blue candy.
You may add a team logo or an initial centered just
above the brim of the hat using blue candies.

Variation: Whip up another cake mix
and make cupcakes. Frost each cooled
cupcake white to look like a baseball
and use a small tube of red frosting
to draw the balls' laces.

rocket blastoff

1. Make cake mix according to package directions. Fill three cups in the cupcake pan about two-thirds full. Pour remaining batter into a well-greased 9 x 13-inch pan. Bake cupcakes and cake at 350 degrees for 20 to 23 minutes and then carefully remove cupcakes from oven. Bake cake another 10 to 15 minutes, or until done. Cool cake in pan for 10 minutes, then invert and cool completely on a wire rack.

2. Cut the cake according to the diagram. Position the wings at the bottom sides of the rocket according to the photo. Frost the entire cake white.

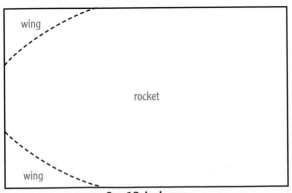

9 x 13-inch pan

PANS: 1 (9 x 13-inch) pan
Cupcake pan

1 cake mix, any flavor

White frosting

Dark blue frosting

Red and blue M&Ms

1 tube red gel frosting or
   red rope licorice

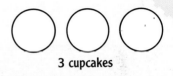

3 cupcakes

SERVES: 10 to 12

3. Slice off the tops of the cupcakes; throw away or eat the bottoms. Frost the cupcake tops and sides blue. Place on the rocket to look like windows. (Make sure the frosting completely covers the sides of the cupcake tops so no cake is showing.)

4. Using red and blue M&Ms, spell out USA on one side of the windows, and make a U.S. flag on the other side.

5. Position more red M&Ms along the bottom sides of the tail wings.

6. Outline entire rocket in red gel frosting or using red rope licorice as seen in the photo.

christmas tree

1. Make cake mix according to package directions. Bake cake as directed on box for a 9 x 13-inch pan. Cool cake in pan for 10 minutes, and then invert and cool completely on a wire rack.

2. Cut the cake according to the diagram. Position the two smaller triangle pieces together to create one large triangle and frost the top green. Place the other triangle on top and frost entire cake green. Place candy bar piece in the center of the flat part of tree to make the trunk.

3. Using a decorator's bag with a star tip, frost a white garland diagonally across the tree like in the photo. Decorate the tree with candy as desired.

Variation: Frost the tree with green mint frosting or sprinkle on shredded coconut that has been tinted green to look like pine needles.

PANS: 1 (9 x 13-inch) pan

1 chocolate cake mix
Green frosting
$1/2$ King-Size Snickers or
   Milky Way candy bar
White frosting
Red candies, like M&Ms,
   striped peppermints, or
   Red Hots

SERVES: 8 to 10

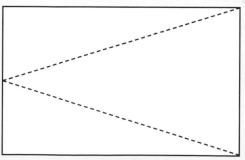

9 x 13-inch pan

caterpillar

PANS: Bundt pan

1 white cake mix

Ingredients listed on cake mix

Green frosting

Purple frosting

Black rope licorice

2 mini Oreos

Black gel frosting

1. Make cake mix according to package directions. Bake cake as directed on box for a Bundt pan. Cool cake in pan for 10 minutes, and then invert and cool completely on a wire rack.

2. Cut the cake according to the diagram. Stand the largest piece on a plate or foil-wrapped board so it makes an arch. Place the other pieces on each side of the arch to create the caterpillar's body. Using some of the frosting, frost the smaller pieces to the arch to secure, then frost the entire cake green.

bundt pan

3. Using a decorator's bag with a star tip, frost green and purple stripes of caterpillar fuzz to look like the photograph.

4. Cut two pieces of licorice rope for the antennae and place in the appropriate position.

SERVES: 10 to 12

5. Use mini Oreo cookies and black gel frosting to make the eyes.

Variation: Use rainbow chip or funfetti cake mix, or add green food coloring to your batter just for fun!

hoppy
the bunny

PANS: 2 (9-inch) round pans

1 cake mix, any flavor

Ingredients listed on cake mix

Pink or lavender frosting

White frosting

M&Ms and Sprees

Red licorice rope or 1 tube red
  gel frosting

Black licorice rope or 1 tube
  black gel frosting

SERVES: 10 to 12

1. Make cake mix according to package directions. Bake cakes as directed on box for two round pans. Cool cakes in pans for 10 minutes, and then invert and cool completely on a wire rack.

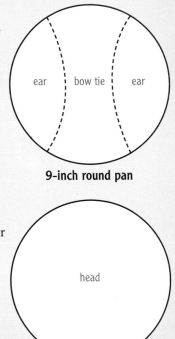

9-inch round pan

9-inch round pan

2. Cut one cake layer according to the diagram and set aside.

3. Place the other cake layer a plate or foil-wrapped board to make the bunny's head. Place the cut ears and bow tie around the bunny's head. Frost the centers of the ears with pink frosting, and

44

then frost the rest of the bunny with white frosting. Frost the bow tie with pink or lavender frosting.

4. Arrange the M&Ms or Sprees on the bow tie to look like polka dots. For the face, use 2 M&Ms for eyes and 1 for the nose.

5. Using your black licorice rope or black tube frosting, draw a line down from the nose and place whiskers on either side of the line. Using red licorice rope or red gel frosting, draw a smile under the whiskers.

Variation: Sprinkle coconut over your bunny before decorating with candy so he looks like he has fur!

slithers the snake

1. Make cake mix with ingredients according to directions on box. Bake cake as directed on box for a Bundt pan. Cool cake in pan for 10 minutes, and then invert and cool completely on a wire rack.

2. Cut the cake in half to make two half-circles. Slide the pieces together so that the cut ends touch and the cake looks like an S. Frost entire cake with bright green frosting.

3. To make the tiered snake tail, cut 1/3 off the bottom of a Ding Dong and discard. Place the Ding Dong, cut side down, at one of the cut ends of the cake. Press into frosting to secure, and then frost green. Cut a second Ding Dong in half and set one half aside. Stand the other half next to the frosted Ding Dong and press to secure, then frost green. Cut a little more off the reserved half and add that to the tail and frost green.

Bundt pan

PANS: Bundt pan

1 yellow or lemon cake mix

Bright green frosting

3 Ding Dongs

1 large white marshmallow

1 tube black gel frosting

Yellow candies like M&Ms, Skittles, or Lemonheads

1 red Fruit by the Foot

SERVES: 10 to 12

47

4. Use the remaining Ding Dong to make the mouth. Cut it in half, and then frost with green frosting. Place one half at the end of the cake opposite the tail with the cut side touching the cut side of the cake. Stick a couple toothpicks near the back and place the second Ding Dong half on top so the mouth looks open. (If it won't stay open, stick some of the yellow candies in the back to prop it open.) Blend the frosting so the mouth looks connected with the cake.

5. Cut the large white marshmallow in half, and place the cut sides into the frosting for the snake's eyes. Secure with toothpicks if necessary. Use the black gel frosting to draw a line from the top to the bottom of each eye.

6. Place yellow candies all over snake to create spots and use more green frosting to secure if necessary.

7. Finally, cut the Fruit by the Foot to resemble a snake's tongue, and place it in the snake's mouth.

chugga chugga choo choo

1. Make cake mix according to package directions. Evenly separate batter into well-greased mini loaf pans. Bake cakes at 350 degrees for 20 to 23 minutes, or until done. Cool cakes in pans for 10 minutes, and then invert and cool completely on a wire rack.

2. Cut one mini cake loaf in half. Position one of the halves on the top of another mini cake loaf on one end to make the engine. Throw away or eat the other half. Place the engine on a plate or foil-wrapped board, followed by the cars to create the train.

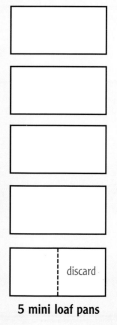

discard

5 mini loaf pans

3. Frost the engine red and then each car a different color. Draw windows on the engine with the white tube frosting. Press 2 Oreos into the frosting on each side of the engine and cars to make the wheels.

PANS: 5 mini loaf pans

1 cake mix, any flavor

Red, orange, and yellow frosting

1 large tube white frosting

1 tube black frosting

16 Oreos

1 plain ice cream cone

Cotton candy (optional)

Candy for decorating cars

SERVES: 8 to 10

4. Frost the ice cream cone black and position on front of engine. (You may need to cut part of the cake away so the cone sits securely.) Place some cotton candy on top to look like smoke.

5. Decorate the engine and cars with the candy of your choice, or use candies shown in photo.

Variation: Use black licorice to connect the cars, as seen in the photo.

pirate ship

1. Make cake mix according to package directions. Bake at 350 degrees F for 39 to 44 minutes, or until done. Test by inserting a wooden skewer in the center; if it comes out clean the cake is done. Cool cake in pan for 10 minutes, and then invert and cool completely on a wire rack.

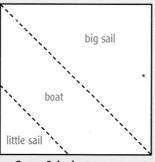

8- or 9-inch square pan

2. Cut the cake according to the diagram.

3. Position the pieces to create the ship and sails. Frost the sails with white frosting and the ship bottom with chocolate frosting. Draw a line of black frosting between the sails, or position black licorice between the sails. Place Lifesavers on ship to look like windows. Cut Fruit by the Foot to resemble a flag and position it at the top of the black frosting or licorice.

PANS: 1 (8- or 9-inch) square pan

1 white, yellow, or chocolate cake mix

White frosting

Chocolate frosting

1 tube black frosting or 1 piece black licorice

5 white Lifesavers

1 Fruit by the Foot

SERVES: 10 to 12

slug bug

PANS: 1 bread pan
      1 (1.5-quart) glass
        mixing bowl

1 cake mix, any flavor

Orange frosting

White frosting

2 white Mentos candies

2 red M&Ms

4 mini chocolate donuts

1. Make cake mix according to package directions. Pour half the batter into a well-greased bread pan and the other half into a well-greased bowl. Bake cakes at 350 degrees F for 34 to 37 minutes, then carefully remove the cake in the bread pan. Bake the cake in the bowl for 5 to 7 minutes more, or until done. Test by inserting a wooden skewer in the center; if it comes out clean the cake is done. Cool cakes in pan and bowl for 10 minutes, and then invert and cool completely on a wire rack.

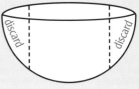

1.5-quart glass mixing bowl

bread pan

2. Place the rectangular cake on a plate or foil-wrapped board. Frost the top orange, then center the bowl cake on top with the flat side down. Cut off the overhanging sides of the bowl cake to create the body of the car. Frost the entire car orange.

SERVES: 8 to 10

3. Frost a white windshield, side windows and rear window on the car.

4. Place the Mentos on the front of the car to look like headlights and the M&Ms in the back to look like brake lights.

5. Position two mini donuts on each side of the car for the tires.

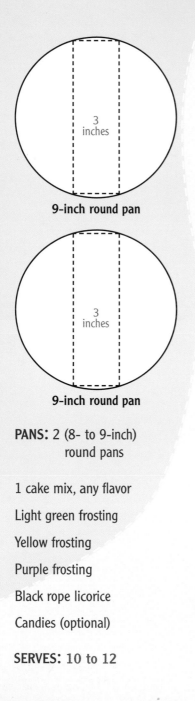

3 inches

9-inch round pan

3 inches

9-inch round pan

PANS: 2 (8- to 9-inch) round pans

1 cake mix, any flavor

Light green frosting

Yellow frosting

Purple frosting

Black rope licorice

Candies (optional)

SERVES: 10 to 12

dragonfly

1. Make cake mix according to package directions. Bake cake as directed on box for two round pans. Cool cakes in pans for 10 minutes, and then invert and cool completely on a wire rack.

2. Cut each cake according to the diagram. Cut a little piece off each end of both long strips to make them square. Place the strips end to end on a plate or foil-wrapped board to make the dragonfly body. Frost body light green. Position the half-circle pieces of cake as wings on either side of the dragonfly's body, as shown in the photo and frost yellow.

3. Decorate the wings using purple frosting and a decorator's bag with a small round tip. Drizzle frosting over the wings in a squiggly pattern. Use a decorator's bag with a star tip to outline the body. Decorate with a few colored candies if desired.

4. Place cut pieces of rope licorice to make the antennae.

Variation: Instead of drizzling frosting on the wings, use decorator's sprinkles.

dandy lion

PANS: 1 (8 x 8 or 9 x 9-inch) square pan

1 cake mix, any flavor

Yellow-gold frosting

Brown frosting

1 small tube black gel frosting

4 pieces black licorice

2 large marshmallows

1 Whopper candy

1 Butterfinger stix

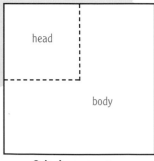

8-inch square pan

SERVES: 10 to 12

1. Make cake mix with ingredients according to directions on box. Bake cake at 350 degrees F for 39 to 44 minutes, or until done. Cool cake in pan for 10 minutes, and then invert and cool completely on a wire rack.

2. Cut the cake according to the diagram.

3. Place the lion's body on a plate or foil-wrapped board. Position the square piece to make the lion's head. Frost the body with the yellow-gold frosting. Using brown frosting in a decorator's bag with a star tip, create the lion's mane. Using the black gel frosting, draw a line to look like the lion's mouth.

4. Cut about $1^1/_2$ inches off the end of each piece of licorice and set aside. Stick the longer pieces of licorice into the cake and position so the lion looks like he is walking. Add the leftover pieces of licorice to create his feet, using frosting to secure, if needed.

5. Cut one marshmallow in half and position as the lion's eye. Use the black gel frosting to create the

center of his eye. Place the Whopper candy in position to create the nose.

6. Frost the remaining marshmallow with yellow-gold frosting and poke Butterfinger stix inside. Position on the back of lion as the tail.

Variation: Use chocolate chips for the mane instead of frosting.

you're my sweetheart

PANS: 1 (8-inch) square pan
1 (8-inch) round pan

1 strawberry cake mix

Pink frosting

1 large tube white frosting

Pastel candies, such as M&Ms,
Skittles, jelly beans, Shock
Tarts, or gum drops

SERVES: 10 to 12

1. Make cake mix according to package directions. Bake cake as directed on box for two pans. Cool cakes in pans for 10 minutes, and then invert and cool completely on a wire rack.

8-inch round pan

2. Place the square cake on a plate or foil-wrapped board diagonally. Cut the round cake in half according to the diagram, and then place cut sides against the top two sides of the square to make a heart.

3. Frost entire cake pink. Outline top and bottom edge with white tube

8-inch square pan

frosting or using white frosting in a decorator's bag with a star tip. Decorate cake with pastel candies of your choice. You can use the candies to create flowers as seen in the photo.

Variation: Frost the cake white instead of pink, and use red tube frosting to outline the edges!

creepy crawly spider

PANS: 2 (8- or 9-inch)
round pans

1 cake mix, any flavor

Black frosting

Purple frosting

8 pieces black licorice

1 large marshmallow

8- or 9-inch round pan

SERVES: 10 to 12

8- or 9-inch round pan

1. Make cake mix according to package directions. Bake cake as directed on box for two round pans. Cool cakes in pans for 10 minutes, then invert and cool completely on a wire rack.

2. Place one cake layer in the center of a plate or foil-wrapped board. Frost the top with black or purple frosting, and then place the second layer over top. Frost the entire cake with a thin layer of black or purple frosting.

3. Using a decorator's bag with a star tip, make black spider hair by slightly squeezing the bag to create each piece of hair. Squeeze pieces of hair close together over the entire body, but don't worry about making them touch, as the spaces will be filled in.

4. Using another decorator's bag with the same star tip, fill in any spaces with the purple

frosting so the spider's hair is highlighted.

5. On each side of the spider, using a round frosting tip, create four rounded mounds of purple frosting. These will be the spider's feet.

6. Gently press 4 pieces of black licorice into each side of the cake to create the spider's legs, and then place the loose ends of licorice into the frosting mounds that are his feet on each side of the cake.

7. Finally, cut the marshmallow in half and place as the spider's eyes. Use a dot of black frosting on each to finish.

About the Author

Melissa Barlow received her bachelor's degree in journalism from Weber State University. She is a freelance writer and editor. She also has formal training in cake decorating. Melissa is co-author of the book *101 Things To Do With a Salad*. She lives with her husband, Todd, in Bountiful, Utah.